Children of
GUATEMALA

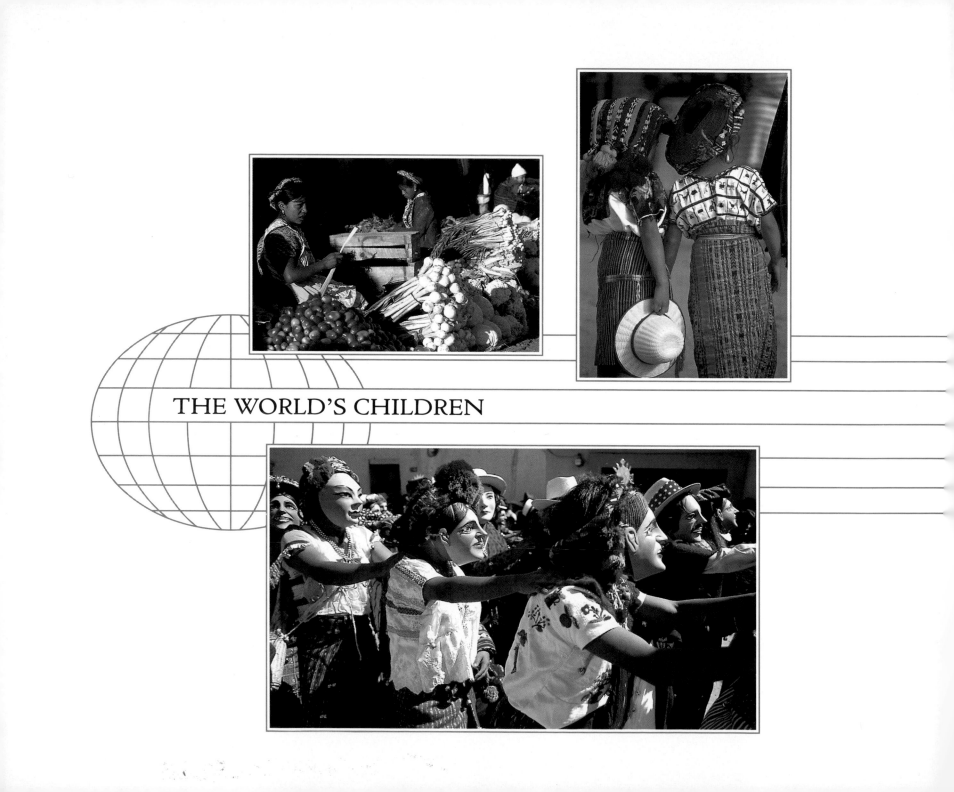

THE WORLD'S CHILDREN

Children of
GUATEMALA

JULES HERMES

Carolrhoda Books, Inc./Minneapolis

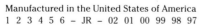
In memory of the missing, and the victims of war everywhere.

I wish to thank the padres of Mission San Lucas Toliman for their kindness, wisdom, and encouragement. I also wish to thank Lisa Torun and United Airlines for their assistance. A special thanks goes to Dr. Manuel Fernández for his generous assistance in the preparation of this book. Finally, I would like to thank the people of Guatemala for sharing their stories of sadness and joy with a stranger.

Text and photographs copyright © 1997 by Jules Hermes.
Illustration copyright © 1997 by Carolrhoda Books, Inc.

Carolrhoda Books, Inc., c/o The Lerner Publishing Group
241 First Avenue North, Minneapolis, MN 55401 U.S.A.

LIBRARY OF CONGRESS CATALOGING-IN-PUBLICATION DATA

Hermes, Jules, 1962–
    Children of Guatemala / by Jules Hermes.
        p.   cm. — (The world's children)
    Includes index.
    Summary: Presents an overview of the history, geography, and people of Guatemala by introducing Mayan, Cakchiquel, Ladino, and Garifuna children.
    ISBN 0-87614-994-8
    1. Guatemala—Social life and customs—Juvenile literature.
2. Children—Guatemala—Social life and customs—Juvenile literature.
[1. Guatemala—Social life and customs.] I. Title. II. Series: World's children (Minneapolis, Minn.)
F1463.2.H47 1997
972.81 — dc20   96-26546

Manufactured in the United States of America
1 2 3 4 5 6 – JR – 02 01 00 99 98 97

Author's Note

As a child in Minnesota, I never paid much attention to what was happening around the world. But as I grew older, I discovered that my clothes could have been sewn by a child in India, the leather in my shoes could have been dyed by a child in Morocco, and my favorite fruits could have been picked by children in Guatemala. Knowing this, I decided to see for myself what life was like for the children there. I thought if I could visit with them and then share what I learned, we might all come to understand one another a little bit better.

I chose to visit Guatemala because I had heard that it is a beautiful but troubled place. Guatemala is the wealthiest country in Central America. More than half the

citizens are Mayan Indians. But the majority of money and land is controlled by a small group of families who are chiefly descendants of the Spanish conquerors. Ever since Guatemala gained independence from Spain in 1821, these families have run the government (except for a brief try at reform during the 1940s and early 1950s). This government has been brutal to citizens who want to share the land more equally or make the government more representative. Now most Maya, as well as people of mixed Mayan and European heritage, struggle to survive on what little land is left. Many in Guatemala live off as little as $250 a year.

Guatemala has suffered through one of the longest civil wars in the world. Thousands of people, mostly Maya, have been kidnapped, tortured, and/or killed by government soldiers. Some have been attacked because they were rebel soldiers, others because they spoke out against the government, and still others because they happened to be in the wrong place at the wrong time.

Even so, as I look back at the photographs of the children I met in Guatemala, I am reminded of how they have learned to cope with these harsh realities. Still happy, still trusting, and always willing to share their lives with a stranger, they made my journey one that I will never forget, and one that I want to share with you.

Deep in the heart of Guatemala's western highlands is the village of Chajul. Here, two Mayan sisters, Maria and Teresa, begin their day before the sun rises. Walking down the dirt road in their village, they hear the clap-clap sounds of women making tortillas—flat, breadlike pancakes.

The girls are on their way to make tortillas for their family. Each morning, they bring their corn to the village *molino,* a motor-driven grinder, where the kernels are ground into flour. With the flour and some water, they make dough and shape it into small disks, then cook them over a hot, cast-iron griddle. For their family of eight, Maria and Teresa make as many as 125 tortillas a day.

As they work, the girls remember an old Mayan legend their grandfather used to tell about the creation of humans. People were created from corn, he said, and to survive, they must grow the corn they eat on their own land. Though Maria and Teresa's family owns just a small plot of land, they try hard to live by this legend.

Corn, seen drying on a roof above, is essential to Maria and Teresa's family, as it is to all Guatemalans. Most Guatemalan diets consist of tortillas, black beans with chilies, vegetables, and occasionally chicken or beef.

Right: *Guatemala is sectioned into twenty-three parts, called* departamentos. *The Ixiles are one of the many groups of Mayan peoples in Guatemala. The largest are the Quiché, Cakchiquel, Kekchi, Mam, and Pocomam. Opposite page: Maria and Teresa are Ixil Maya from the* departamento *of Quiché, in the highlands.*

BELIZE

• Tikal

• Flores

MEXICO

GUATEMALA

Cuchumatanes Mountains

Livingston

Todos los Santos

• Chajul

San Francisco el Alto

• Momostenango

Quetzaltenango

• Chichicastenango

HONDURAS

Zunil

• Guatemala City

Retalhuleu •

Esquipulas

•Antigua

Santiago Atitlán

San Lucas Tolimán

EL SALVADOR

NORTH AMERICA

ATLANTIC OCEAN

GUATEMALA

SOUTH AMERICA

PACIFIC OCEAN

PACIFIC OCEAN

KEY

departamento boundary

mountain range

ruins

As early as 600 B.C., the Maya lived throughout Central America. Around A.D. 300, they began to build cities with magnificent palaces and temples. Then the Spanish arrived in the 1500s and ruled for three centuries. They enslaved the Maya, took away most of their land, and even tried to force them to give up their beliefs and traditions to become Catholic. But the Maya secretly resisted, passing down many parts of their heritage through the generations.

In the lush rain forests of northern Guatemala is Tikal, the ruins of a great Mayan city. Victoria and her two cousins Rosa and Raúl are visiting this famous site. They come from Flores, a large tourist town just thirty minutes from Tikal.

Victoria's family made their wealth in the tourism industry, and she is proud of their Spanish heritage. "The Mayans built the ancient cities," she says, "but we built Guatemala's modern cities."

Like others of the wealthy class, Victoria does not have any Mayan friends because she does not go to school with them or speak their languages. She goes to an expensive private school with other children of Spanish descent, and her home is guarded by security police.

Opposite page: *The ancient Maya also lived with big differences between the rich and the poor. The great stone temples of Tikal were built by poor Maya, who were governed by rich Mayan priests and lords.*

Victoria

9

Most Spanish Guatemalans live in the larger cities and follow the latest trends in music, entertainment, and fashions. In contrast, most Maya live in the highland villages, follow their centuries-old customs, and speak their native languages.

The Maya also tend to wear colorful handwoven *traje,* or traditional clothing. Each village has its own colors and patterns of cloth that the women and young girls weave by hand.

Sotero and Luciano are two young Mam Maya who proudly wear the striped pants and shirts of their village, Todos los Santos Cuchumatán. This little hamlet is nestled among the Cuchumatanes Mountains, over ten thousand feet above sea level. Little has changed in Todos los Santos over the last hundred years.

Sotero and Luciano, wearing the traje *of Todos los Santos, get a shoeshine from a young boy named Santiago. Some believe the Maya were forced to wear* traje *by the Spanish, who used the distinct clothing to identify the village of their "human property."*

Some cloth sold to be used for women's skirts

It takes three hours by bus or car to reach Todos los Santos from the nearest city. Steep, twisting dirt roads make travel in and out of the village very difficult, especially during the wind-whipped, chilly winters. Some people living in the mountains around the village must walk up to twelve miles on weekly market days to buy and sell their wares and produce.

Once called the "land of eternal spring," Guatemala has a varied, springlike climate. The western highlands, as in Todos los Santos (above right), have cold, foggy mornings with sunny, warm afternoons. But during their winter season, they may see frost and occasional snow. As the land becomes lower, the temperatures become warmer. The northern rain forests and the southern highlands around Lake Atitlán (right) enjoy temperate weather, averaging seventy-five degrees during the day. Along the coastlands, it is hot and humid but kept pleasant by sea winds.

Ladinos like Joel are easily identified in Todos los Santos because they wear store-bought clothing rather than traditional traje, *and they speak Spanish. Joel also speaks a little Mam, the language of the Maya of Todos los Santos.*

Opposite page: *Instead of having stores, each town and village in the Guatemalan highlands has its own market held on a specific day of the week, and each town has its own specialty product. Markets offer villagers everything from handmade furniture to livestock.* Opposite page inset: *The Todos los Santos market*

In preparation for this week's market, twelve-year-old Joel drains the blood from a slaughtered sheep his family will sell. With the blood drained, the animal weighs less and is easier to carry. Todos los Santos is famous for its blood sausages.

Joel and his family are among the very few Ladinos living in Todos los Santos. Ladinos are Guatemalans of mixed Mayan and European heritage. Most Ladinos live in Guatemala City or the coastal and eastern lowlands. However, Joel and his family choose to remain in the highlands because they believe this is the best region for raising animals.

Julián wears the round straw hat that is typical of his village.

Nine-year-old Julián is a Mam who also lives in Todos los Santos. During the Friday market, Julián roams the cobblestone streets. He stops to talk to his young friend, Nosario, who is helping his mother at his family's hat stand.

Julián's favorite pastime is to stop by a local restaurant to watch the televisions mounted on the wall. Most of the programs are in Spanish, Guatemala's official language. Julián understands very little Spanish, but he likes to watch the moving pictures and listen to the music and the voices.

A rare sight in the more remote villages of Guatemala—televisions

Nosario sits with his brother and sister at the hat stand his family owns.

Julián will only attend school until he is old enough to help his father and brothers in the fields. That means he will probably drop out in the fourth grade. A great number of children never go to school, even though the law says they should. Their families cannot afford the school fees and need many helping hands on the farm.

Sara also lives in the western highlands. The closest town to her home is San Francisco el Alto, meaning "the high one." Like Todos los Santos, San Francisco hosts a huge weekly market. Thousands of people gather to buy and sell livestock.

On Fridays before dawn, Sara and her mother set out with their sheep for the market. Sitting crouched in the back of a small, covered pickup, Sara and her mother and several sheep ride two hours through the cold morning. The truck stops twice to pick up more villagers who wait by burning fires along the roadside with their livestock. They reach the market at 6:00 A.M., and one by one the villagers and animals climb out, stretching their cramped muscles.

Opposite page: *The highlands are the best place to raise sheep because there are trees and plenty of open grassland for grazing.*

Sara and her mother arrive at the market with their sheep.

Manuela makes fresh corn tortillas, bread, and chuchitos *to sell.*

The market in San Francisco is well underway by 7:00 A.M. Villagers warm themselves with coffee and hot tortillas. Thirteen-year-old Manuela and her mother run a food stall where they sell fresh bread, coffee, corn tortillas, and *chuchitos*—small dumplings made of corn flour and lard, and filled with a meat and tomato sauce.

One of these huge, typical breakfasts sells for three *quetzales,* or about fifty cents. The *quetzal* is a Guatemalan coin that gets its name from the quetzal bird, which lives in northeastern Guatemala.

Villagers walk along the steep road to the market in San Francisco el Alto. The market offers a break from everyday work and gives friends a chance to catch up on the latest news.

Manuela's younger brother, Diego, carries their baby brother on his back while Manuela and her mother serve food. Children as young as five years old often take care of the little ones in the family while one or both of their parents work in the market.

19

Sevillio comes from Momostenango, a small town tucked in a thick pine forest not far from San Francisco el Alto. People here still use an ancient Mayan calendar with a 260-day year. Because their years are shorter, Sevillio has more birthdays than most children. He is fourteen years old by our calendar, but by his Mayan calendar, he is almost twenty.

Sevillio is a wool trader in Momostenango, Guatemala's wool capital. Twice weekly, Sevillio arrives in the town square, where he and his family buy enormous bundles of wool from villagers who raise sheep. Though he has had no formal education, Sevillio understands the different kinds of wool and judges the best uses and costs for each. He is experienced at getting the highest prices for the wool he sells.

The wool at Momostenango is often sold to local women who dye it and then weave with it. Many of the wool blankets, rugs, and pieces of clothing made in Guatemala will be sold around the world.

A blanket trader checks the quality of the wool blankets at the Momostenango market. Blanket traders often go from market to market in the highlands before choosing the ones they want. These they will sell around the world.

After the flurry of activity on market days, things quiet down in the highland villages—until Mass on Sunday morning. Most Guatemalans are Roman Catholic, though many practice a mix of Christianity and their ancient religion. The Mayan gods guide them in farming and other work, while the Christian saints guide them in family life. Every Guatemalan town has a patron saint with a special *fiesta,* or celebration, to honor it.

Sebastian lives to the southeast of Momostenango, in Chichicastenango, home to one of Guatemala's most elaborate religious celebrations. Each year on December 21, the town hosts the Fiesta de San Tomás, or the Feast of St. Thomas. To honor this patron saint of Chichicastenango, people from all over the region come to dance and party throughout the day and night. The leaders of the festivities are called *cofradías.* They are part of a secretive religious group that plays an important role in Mayan life.

Hundreds of people gather on the church steps to watch the festivities.

Above: *Sebastian plays the role of the bull in the Danza de los Toritos, or Dance of the Little Bulls.*

Left: *During the Fiesta de San Tomás, processions take place with* cofradías *parading life-size statues of saints through the streets. The* cofradías *wear cloaks made of* quetzales *given by parishioners.*

Huge crowds gather to watch men perform the Danza de las Mujeres, a dance done merely for the laughter and fun of it.

Sebastian's favorite dance is the Danza de las Mujeres, or Dance of the Women. The dance is performed in the streets by men who dress in the *traje* of women and men from different Mayan villages.

One of the most popular dances of the festival is the Danza de la Conquista, or Dance of the Conquest. Sebastian explains that it tells the story of how the Mayan warriors fell under the hands of the Spaniards. When the Maya in this village perform the dance, they mock the Spanish soldiers and make them look like fools.

The Danza de la Conquista

Maya, Ladinos, and foreigners alike come to Chichicastenango to take part in the *fiesta*. Many also make a special pilgrimage to the nearby shrine of a Mayan god called Pascual Abaj. Next to the shrine sits the cross of Christianity. Sebastian, like many Maya, accepts the cross as a Mayan symbol as well as a Christian symbol. It represents the four directions: north, east, south, and west.

Elaine, a six-year-old who lives just a hundred steps from the shrine of Pascual Abaj, sells miniature masks. They have been made by her father for tourists and pilgrims. The pilgrims traditionally offer chickens and other animals to Pascual Abaj.

Encarnación lives in the village of Zunil, in the west central highlands. Her father, Pedro, works hard on a *finca,* or large plantation. Most *fincas* are owned by wealthy Guatemalan families of European heritage.

When Encarnación was a small child, her father had to pick one hundred pounds of coffee beans per day on the *finca.* This sometimes took twelve or thirteen hours, and he was paid only one *centavo* (worth less than a penny) for each pound. If Pedro broke a branch, he had to pay the lord of the *finca* for the damage. He saw many of his family members die from the hardships of this life on the *finca.*

Over the last decades, things have improved a little. Many Maya and Ladinos have been forming workers' groups, or unions, to demand fairer laws, better working conditions, and higher wages. Owners of *fincas* are now required to provide schools for the workers' children. However, changes are coming slowly, and people who speak out for improvements are often in danger.

Left: *Life is getting better for Pedro and others like him, a little at a time. In the past, workers on the* fincas, *who were usually Mayan, were treated like slaves. They lived in cramped and dirty quarters and were paid so little that it was impossible to leave the* finca *for long periods of time.* Above: *Encarnación*

Villagers gather at the hot springs near Zunil where they wash clothes and bathe.

Women from the highlands near Zunil carry produce on their backs to the weekly market in town.

Not all Maya and Ladinos in Guatemala are landless. Sixteen-year-old Guillermo lives in the town of San Lucas Tolimán, on the shores of Lake Atitlán in the southern highlands. Here, more and more people are beginning to acquire small plots of land. Guillermo's family owns no land, but he works for a Mayan land-owner picking coffee beans.

After the beans are harvested, Guillermo delivers them to a local mill where the beans are dried, packaged, and shipped to other countries. Guillermo says the best beans are sold overseas, while poorer-quality beans are sold in Guatemala. Most Guatemalans cannot afford to drink good-quality coffee, because a pound of any first-class coffee beans costs more than most pickers make in one day.

Carefully, Guillermo picks coffee beans from a grove on a hillside high above the town of San Lucas Tolimán. Here, the high altitude and volcanic soil provide excellent conditions for growing coffee.

Right: *Coffee has become one of the top crops of Guatemala. Most coffee plantations are still in the hands of a few wealthy landowners. Much of Guatemala's fruit, vegetable, and coffee crops are sold in more developed countries.*

Volcanoes surround Lake Atitlán. Guatemala has over two dozen volcanoes, some of them active.

Juan lives in the village of Santiago Atitlán, which is also on the shores of Lake Atitlán. Juan attends a village school, but during the vacation months, he goes with his father to work.

Juan's father works for a wealthy family, tending their fields and making sure the grounds around their enormous home are secure. After work, he and Juan return to their one-room home of wood and tin.

Graves of those killed in the 1990 massacre

A copy of the president's letter engraved in stone in Santiago Atitlán

The community of Santiago Atitlán is different from all other communities in Guatemala. In 1991, the people there declared self-rule. From this point on, the villagers have tried to make their own rules and be independent from the government of Guatemala.

The declaration came after a massacre in Santiago in 1990. During a surprise raid by the Guatemalan military, twelve citizens were killed because they were suspected of fighting against the government. This kind of terror is common in Guatemala.

But after the 1990 massacre, the government of Guatemala promised the villagers that nothing like this would ever happen to them again. To make sure this promise was kept, the villagers of Santiago had the president's letter engraved in a stone near the cemetery where the dead were buried. Due to self-rule, Santiago Atitlán is at peace.

The villages around Lake Atitlán are very popular among tourists because the lake is one of Guatemala's most beautiful natural sites. Many of these tourists come from Guatemala City and Antigua. Antigua was originally Guatemala's capital, but it was devastated by an earthquake in 1773. The new capital was built in Guatemala City, thirty miles away.

Antigua is a relaxed, peaceful town where the ruins of old Spanish churches and monasteries still stand. Many foreigners come to the picturesque city to learn Spanish, and some come to vacation. Most everyone buys souvenirs, so the competition among vendors to make a sale is fierce.

Above right: *By night, the central plaza of Antigua softly glows from lights in the fountain and the trees. Guatemalans as well as visitors gather in the plaza to watch the world go by.* Right: *Children and adults play* futbol, *or soccer, in the shadow of the volcanoes surrounding Antigua.*

Candelaria at the city square. Some of the souvenirs she sells are expensive, but most cost just a few quetzales.

Hand-woven belts sold by Candelaria and her mother

Many Maya from the villages around Antigua come to the city to sell fruits and vegetables they've grown or things they've made. Eight-year-old Candelaria rides the bus each morning from her village to the city square with her mother and brothers. They sell souvenirs such as small carpets, woven bracelets, and belts.

The city of Guatemala has all the conveniences of any large city in the world. Shops line the streets and cars clog the roads.

A mariachi band, a typical Guatemalan musical group, waits outside a restaurant where they will play for the evening.

In contrast to Antigua, Guatemala City—the largest, most modern city in Central America—is crowded and polluted. Here, professionals such as lawyers, doctors, and dentists set up their businesses. Most of Guatemala's wealthy citizens live in the capital city, in mansions behind gates guarded around the clock.

Antonio also lives in Guatemala City. Like thousands and thousands of Guatemalan youth, Antonio must work the streets to earn the few coins he has in his pocket. He calls himself the Fire Eater.

Antonio carries with him a burning stick and a bottle of gasoline. Every few minutes, he takes a swig from the bottle. He does not swallow the gasoline but spits it at the flames, making them explode into a great burst of fire. Then he pushes the stick into his mouth and puts the flames out with his tongue.

After his performance, Antonio walks through the audience that has gathered and collects a few centavos. Though this act is burning his mouth and ruining his health, it is the only way Antonio has found to earn enough money to buy food.

Anna Marsalis was born in a small Mayan village in southeastern Guatemala, but her family moved to Guatemala City when she was a baby. They hoped to find a better life. Her father works odd jobs in the city whenever he can. Her mother sells *chuchitos* and tamales (seasoned meat wrapped in cornmeal dough and corn husks and then steamed) on the streets. Anna helps her mother in the afternoons after she finishes school.

Anna Marsalis and her brothers and sisters feel they have a better chance for a good education in Guatemala City than in the village where they were born. But even in the city there are problems. Books and equipment are scarce, and buildings are falling apart. Teachers often go on strike, demanding better pay, and children join them, pleading for better schools. More often than not, their voices are not heard, and the public schools just get worse.

Teachers and students protest to the government for better schools.

Though the majority of Guatemalans live in the highlands or the large central cities, there are lively communities on both the Pacific and Caribbean coasts. The local people of these regions make a living mainly through farming or food processing.

Manuel lives in Retalhuleu, a city of mostly Ladino people, located near the Pacific Coast in southern Guatemala. Manuel's family owns several small fruit and vegetable stands.

Early in the morning, before school, Manuel helps his father unload fresh produce from trucks. The trucks bring the crops from other parts of Guatemala. After school, Manuel returns to help his family sell the fruit.

Left: *Manuel sells fresh fruit juice at his family-owned stand.* Opposite page: *The city center of Retalhuleu*

Opposite page: *Trenio, Marvin, and Marcello. The boys speak Spanish with Juan Ramos, but at most other times, they speak their Garifuna language. They also follow their own traditions and religious beliefs.*

Juan Ramos and his father fish from their boat.

In contrast to the busy and crowded Pacific coast, much of the Caribbean coast remains quiet and unspoiled. Eleven-year-old Juan Ramos comes from the little town of Livingston. The village is near the border of Belize and can be reached only by boat and airplane. Livingston is home to mostly Ladinos, like Juan Ramos, and to Afro-Garifuna people, also known as the Black Caribes.

Juan Ramos lives in a bamboo hut on the beach that looks out to the Caribbean Sea. He and his father fish the waters for the family supper.

Originally from Western Africa, the ancestors of the Garifunas were captured and taken aboard Portuguese slave ships in 1675. The ships capsized in a storm near the tiny Caribbean island of Saint Vincent of the Lesser Antilles. The Africans swam to shore. Nearly a hundred years later, their descendants were sent away by the British to the eastern coast of Central America. This was the beginning of Livingston, a town the Garifunas call La Buga.

Though the Garifunas and the Ladinos tend to live in separate parts of town, they get along well with each other. Three of Juan's close friends are Garifunas: Marvin, Trenio, and Marcello. The boys all have fishing in common, for that is how their families earn a living.

Despite the anger and separation between some of the different groups in Guatemala, people have managed to find a time and place when everyone can gather together in peace. In the second week of January, the Feast of the Black Christ takes place in Esquipulas, a small town near the Honduras border, in southeastern Guatemala. This is considered one of the biggest celebrations in all of Central America.

Soledad, a nine-year-old boy from Quetzaltenango, one of Guatemala's largest western cities, has traveled all the way across the country with his family and other members of his church to see and touch the Black Christ. This, they feel, will bring them blessings in the year to come.

The story of the Black Christ dates back to the late 1500s, when the Spanish were trying to make the Maya become Catholic. The priests in the area found that the Maya were put off by their church's white-faced statue. So the priests covered the white face with brown stain, which turned black over time. Since the Maya had a dark god named Ek Ahau, they now took a liking to the statue. Soon, it was reported that the Black Christ was performing miracles. Through the ages, these miracle stories multiplied, and to this day, pilgrims add their own tales of answered prayers.

Soledad sits with his family inside the candlelit basilica. The basilica has been cleared to make room for all the people. Because the trip to Esquipulas is very costly, Soledad and his family will sleep in a makeshift tent on the lawn outside the basilica along with thousands of other families. Most have been saving money nearly all year to make this journey.

Soledad looks around. Gathered in one place is the heart and soul of his country—Maya, Ladinos, Garifunas, and Spanish Guatemalans all bound together by the faith, history, and land they share. At a time such as this, it is possible to imagine a better future for Guatemala, one lightened by peace.

Pronunciation Guide

Cakchiquel kah-chee-KELL
centavos sen-TAH-vohs
chuchitos choo-CHEE-tohs
cofradías COH-frah-DEE-ahs
conquista cone-KEES-tah
danza DAHN-sah
departamentos day-par-tah-MEN-tohs
fiesta fee-ES-tah
finca FEEN-kah
futbol foot-BOHL
Ixil ee-SHEEL
Kekchi kehk-CHEE
Mam MAHM
molino moh-LEE-noh
mujeres moo-HAY-res
Pocomam poh-coh-MAHM
quetzales KAYT-zah-lays
Quiché kee-CHAY
toritos toh-REE-tohs
traje TRAH-hay

More about Guatemala's Struggles

Many of the children shown in this book have sadly been touched by Guatemala's civil war. Since 1978, nearly 80,000 Maya have been brutally murdered by their own government. Among the dead are Maria and Teresa's father, grandfather, and uncle, who were murdered in a massacre in their village. Throughout the country, more than 60,000 men, women, and children have been classified as "disappeared" or kidnapped.

Guatemalans are tired of the war. Talks have been ongoing between the government and rebel fighters. At the end of April 1996, a cease-fire began. Then on December 29, 1996, a treaty was signed between the government and the rebel forces. Everyone hopes that these actions can lead to more significant changes and a chance for peace in Guatemala.

Index